NEW MEXICO SANTOS

*Religious Images
in the Spanish New World*

BY E. BOYD
ILLUSTRATIONS BY FRANCES BREESE
EDITED AND WITH A FOREWORD BY YVONNE LANGE, PH.D.

MUSEUM OF NEW MEXICO PRESS • SANTA FE

The examples reproduced here are from the collections of the Archdiocese of Santa Fe, the Taylor Museum in Colorado Springs, and from the private collections of Bobby Berg, Charles D. Carroll, Norma Fiske Day, and Mr. and Mrs. Alan C. Vedder. All others are from the collections of the Museum of New Mexico.

Project editor: Mary Wachs
Design and production: David Skolkin
Typeset in Cochin with Albertus Display
Manufactured in the United States of America
10 9 8 7 6 5 4 3 2 1

Museum of New Mexico Press
Post Office Box 2087
Santa Fe, New Mexico 87504
ISBN: 0–89013–284–4

• N E W   M E X I C O   S A N T O S •

· THE FRANCISCAN SHIELD ·

The crossed arms symbolize Christ and Saint Francis of Assisi. This emblem is found on altar screens in the New Mexico churches of Ranchos de Taos, Trampas, and the Santuario de Chimayó.

• F O R E W O R D •

The reputation of E. (Elizabeth) Boyd (1903–1974) as the pioneer in the scholarly study of the material culture of Hispanic New Mexico is unassailable. Her deep appreciation for its Christian art rested on her training as a fine artist at the Pennsylvania Academy of Fine Arts, Philadelphia, and as an art historian at the Ecole de la Grande Chaumière in Paris. But since 1966, when E. Boyd wrote the text for this publication, originally entitled *New Mexico Santos: How to Name Them*, her careful research has been superseded in some areas by new evidence. For instance, engravings were far less important as a source of inspiration for the *santeros* than were the popular devotional lithographic prints with which European commercial printers flooded worldwide markets in the nineteenth century after the invention of lithography in 1798 and the advent of industrialization. Another case is that of the

Christ Child of Atocha. He is now recognized as having Mexican rather than Spanish roots. What she thought to be El Santo Niño Perdido (Jesus found in the Temple among the doctors) on the basis of oral tradition is really only a manikin to be adorned with garments. Yet another example is the centurion San Acacio, which, it should be noted, was transformed into an army general by German artists. Accordingly, those necessary changes that have been made in this updated edition were warranted by new research and by the need to provide more accurate translations from Spanish into English.

It is remarkable that, with so few iconographic tools available to her, E. Boyd achieved such accuracy in her identification of devotional figures that adorned mission churches and the households of pious Hispanic settlers. Many individuals still seek to find out "What saint is this?" It is for their use that a listing of books of reference on Christian iconography is to be found at the end of this publication.

YVONNE LANGE, 1995

Director Emerita
Museum of International Folk Art
Santa Fe, New Mexico

What saint is this?" is a question asked countless times by owners and students of New Mexican *santos*. Standard references on Christian iconography are not often helpful except for those published in Spain or Spanish-speaking countries. Those published in English, French, or German tend to ignore Spanish cults and advocations. To identify a statue image accredited by local devotees with miraculous powers is even more complicated. These were originally of a universal subject, such as a crucifix or the Virgin. When their shrines became pilgrimage centers for miracle-seeking crowds, they received the name of their town or village, such as the Christ of Esquipulas or Chalma or Mapimi or Our Lady of Pueblito or San Juan de los Lagos. Since New Mexico imagemakers were folk artists, they simplified or omitted many details of dress and attributes that might identify a particular religious image elsewhere.

Important keys to recognizing New Mexican saints are engravings that folk artists found in missals and prayer books printed at the Plantin Press in Antwerp, then in Flanders and now in Belgium, which had exclusive privileges from successive popes and kings of Spain to supply religious books to all Hispanic countries for nearly three hundred years. The engravers working for the press redrew popular masterworks in a broadly Flemish style whether they were by Italian or northern artists. Similiar books and broadsides printed in Mexico City, Guadalajara, or Puebla often featured colonial statue images and also Spanish saints such as Santiago (Saint James Major), patron of Spain; Saint Isidore the Farmer, patron of Madrid; the apparition of the Christ Child to prisoners at Atocha; and the successive appearances of the Virgin of Guadalupe to the Indian Juan Diego near Mexico City in 1531.

Folk artists of New Mexico in the eighteenth and nineteenth centuries took their subject matter from these small-scale prints, discarding rococo details to concentrate on their major themes. They invented their own color schemes or took them from the few polychromed statues or canvases shipped north from New Spain. For lack of gilding other colors were substituted. The results were our New Mexico *santos*: wooden panels (*retablos*) or carved figures (*bultos*) covered with home-prepared gesso and painted in water-soluble pigments. The subjects were chosen by the patron or customer according to his personal devotions. The *santo* or holy image was not an idol, as was claimed by many Protestant visitors to New Mexico a century ago, but only a symbol of the invisible power or holy personage to whom an individual's prayers were addressed. A community aware of this viewpoint could, and did, accept almost abstract images without anatomical realism or perspective. The folk artist emphasized symbols, usually one symbol that, to his patrons, identified the particular image. Attention was directed to the face, which received the most care in carving and coloring in every *bulto* or *retablo*. As a result, many *santos* seem to look far beyond us into a mystic vision unseen by mere humans.

The aim of the drawings presented here is to help collectors and students recognize the most popular and often-found subjects among New Mexico *santos*. The drawings by Frances Breese have been labors of love and are faithful in detail, as well as in spirit, to the originals. Examples shown were chosen from many comparable ones because they are typical of their kind, in good condition, and especially charming. Unfortunately, statues that have been broken, plaster patched, and overpainted and that have lost their attributes or had wrong ones added to them cannot often be correctly identified. *Santos* of New Mexico have in the past been misnamed by persons unfamiliar with either standard Christian iconography or that of Spain and Mexico. Once in print, misnomers persist and add to the general confusion. New Mexicans addressed themselves to Franciscan saints, as a rule, but there are always exceptions to every rule, which explains the presence of saints preferred by other orders. We must also remember that a folk artist might present a familiar image in untraditional dress, color, or unexpected attribute. However, when a New Mexico *santo* is found that is not included in these drawings it may safely be classed as uncommon if not unique.

E. BOYD, 1966

• N E W   M E X I C O   S A N T O S •

· SAINT ACACIUS ·
SAN ACACIO

*A legendary soldier martyr. Dressed in military uniform, he is shown
crucified with his army for being a Christian.*

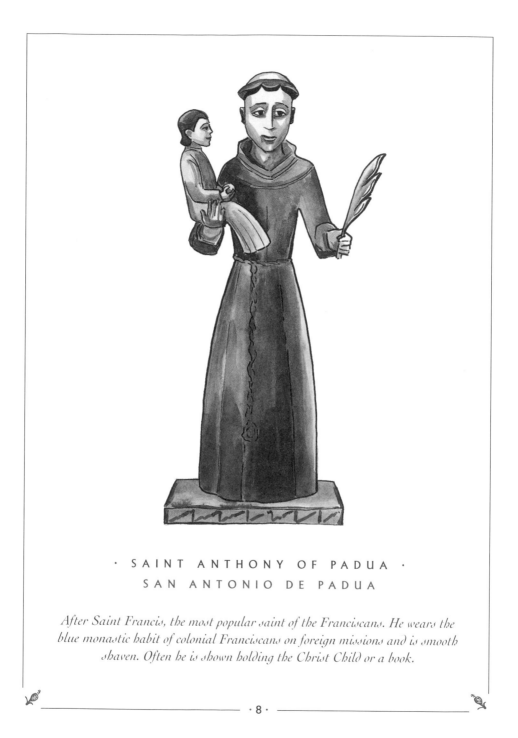

· SAINT ANTHONY OF PADUA ·
SAN ANTONIO DE PADUA

After Saint Francis, the most popular saint of the Franciscans. He wears the blue monastic habit of colonial Franciscans on foreign missions and is smooth shaven. Often he is shown holding the Christ Child or a book.

· SAINT BARBARA ·
SANTA BÁRBARA

An early Christian martyr; shown in a three-tiered skirt and plumed crown, holding a palm and monstrance. Usually depicted with a thundercloud, lightning, and the tower in which she was imprisoned.

· SAINT CAJETAN ·
SAN CAYETANO (CALLETANO)

A founder of the Theatine Order and patron of the sick and poor.
He wears a black cassock with a jeweled collar, is sometimes kneeling by an
altar or sometimes crucified.

· SAINT CHRISTOPHER ·
SAN CRISTÓBAL

*Patron of travelers; he is shown as a barelegged giant bearing the
Christ Child across a river..*

· CRUCIFIX ·
WITH CUPBEARING ANGEL

The small angel often has become separated from the side of a crucifix.
The symbolic theme of angels catching the crucified Christ's blood in a chalice
first appeared in the fourteenth century.

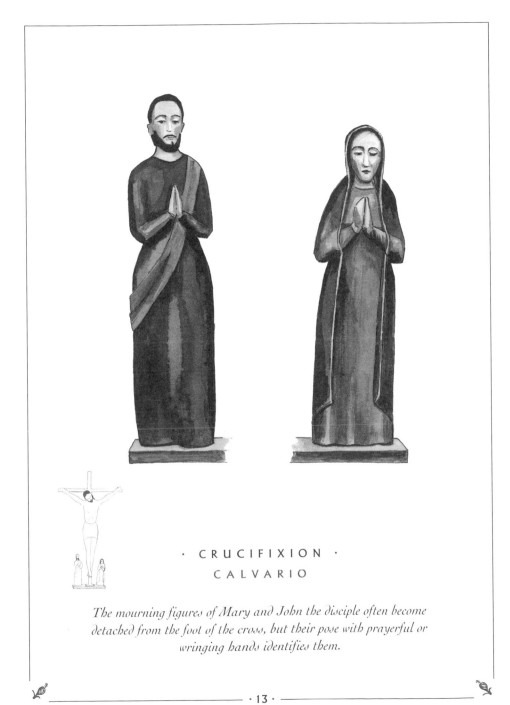

· C R U C I F I X I O N ·
C A L V A R I O

*The mourning figures of Mary and John the disciple often become
detached from the foot of the cross, but their pose with prayerful or
wringing hands identifies them.*

· SAINT FRANCIS OF ASSISI ·
SAN FRANCISCO DE ASÍS

The founder of the Franciscan Order, he wears a blue habit and a beard;
as a rule he holds a cross and skull and has the marks of the stigmata on
his hands and feet.

· SAINT FRANCIS XAVIER ·
SAN FRANCISCO XAVIER

*The great missionary of the Jesuit Order to the Orient; he is shown in
black robes and biretta holding a cross and palm.*

· GABRIEL THE ARCHANGEL ·
SAN GABRIEL ARCÁNGEL

*Gabriel is distinguished from other archangels by the monstrance
or chalice that he holds.*

· SAINT GERTRUDE THE GREAT ·
SANTA GERTRUDIS LA GRANDE

She wears a black nun's habit and holds a crozier and heart. Her mystical writings have been compared with those of Saint Theresa of Avila; they deal with devotion to the Heart of Jesus. Gertrude was declared patroness of Spanish America.

· MANIKIN TO BE ADORNED WITH GARMENTS ·
IMAGEN DE VESTIR

*Two figures of this type are to be found in the church of San Antonio de Padua,
Córdova, New Mexico. (Formerly inaccurately identified as El Santo Niño Perdido,
Jesus found in the Temple among the doctors.)*

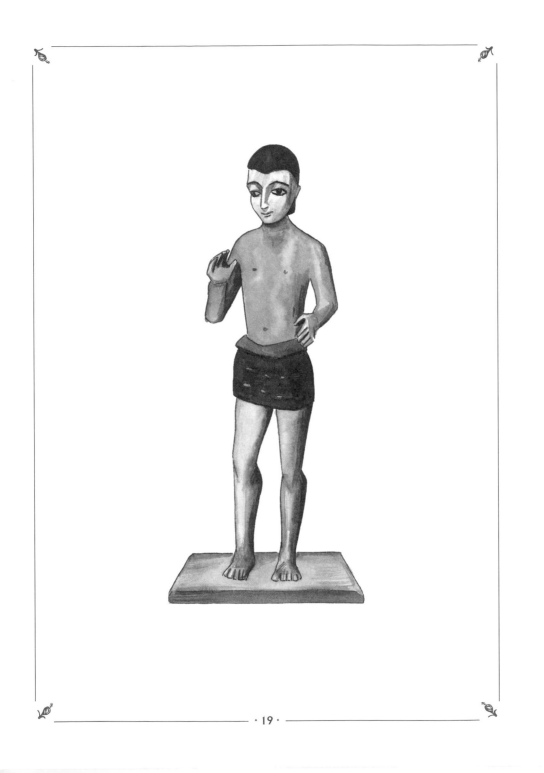

· THE CHRIST CHILD OF ATOCHA ·
EL SANTO NIÑO DE ATOCHA

A Mexican image referring to the apparition of the Christ Child to Christian prisoners in a Moorish dungeon at Atocha near Madrid. He is shown in pilgrim dress and cocked hat with a gourd of water and basket of bread from which he gave real and spiritual nourishment to the prisoners. Sometimes he is shown with leg irons symbolizing the prisoners who invoke his aid.

· THE CHRIST CHILD OF THE NATIVITY ·
EL SANTO NIÑO DE NAVIDAD

The infant Christ in the manger was placed on the altar on Christmas Eve in New Mexico but without the attendant figures, shepherds, and animals made in Italy, Spain, or Mexico.

· THE INFANT JESUS OF PRAGUE ·
EL SANTO NIÑO DE PRAGA

Originally a small statue taken to Prague by a Spanish princess when she married a Bohemian king, it survived the destruction of a chapel by fire during Lutheran ravages. Later regarded as miracle working, the figure, in New Mexico, wears a red robe and holds a cross and blue orb.

· THE HOLY TRINITY ·
LA SANTÍSIMA TRINIDAD

Representation of the Father, Son, and Holy Ghost as three identical persons had been common in European art until it was banned about 1560 but persisted in Spanish Colonial art until recently. The mystery was also portrayed by folk artists with God the Father holding the crucified Christ and the Holy Spirit hovering above. This depiction is known as the Throne of Grace.

· THE HOLY FAMILY ·
LA SAGRADA FAMILIA

*The Christ Child walking between Mary and Joseph, often but not always
in red robes. Some retablos depict God the Father and the dove,
representing the Holy Ghost, appearing above the Child in a vertical Trinity.*

Always modeled after the picture in the basilica of Guadalupe in Mexico City, which is said to have been miraculously painted on the garment of the Indian Juan Diego, to whom the Virgin appeared four times in 1531. She wears a red gown, star-strewn blue cloak, and is surrounded by a nimbus of flames. At her feet are a cherub and the crescent moon. The name Guadalupe comes from the shrine of a much older miraculous statue of the Virgin in Estremadura, Spain.

· SAINT IGNATIUS LOYOLA ·
SAN IGNACIO DE LOYOLA

The founder of the Jesuit Order wears black robes and biretta, or is shown as bald after a contemporary portrait, and holds a radiating disk or a plaque bearing the letters IHS.

· OUR LADY OF THE
IMMACULATE CONCEPTION ·
Nstra Sra DE LA PURÍSIMA CONCEPCIÓN

*Images of Mary in white with blue drapery, usually a crown of roses on her
head and cherubs at her feet, symbolize her immaculate birth wherein she
was free from original sin.*

· SAINT ISIDORE THE FARMER ·
SAN YSIDRO LABRADOR

He wears a blue coat and breeches, red vest, and flat-crowned hat, which was the dress of New Mexican colonial farmers. He drives a team of oxen pulling an old-style wooden plow; sometimes with an angel beside him. Legends tell that his desire to pray in the fields of his master was rewarded by an angel coming to drive his team for him. He is patron of Madrid and of New Mexico farmers.

· SAINT JAMES MAJOR ·
SANTIAGO

The patron of Spain, his shrine is at Compostela. Apparitions of the militant apostle during battles with the Moors in Spain were said to have brought victory to the Spaniards. In the New World no less than fourteen apparitions of Santiago in battles between Spanish and Indians are recorded. One of these was in aid of Oñate during the attack on Acoma Pueblo in New Mexico in 1599. Santos of Santiago usually show him in the military dress of the conquistadors but others depict that of the late eighteenth century. His horse also has trappings of the conquest period and tramples infidels under its hooves.

· SAINT JEROME ·
SAN GERÓNIMO

One of the four doctors of the Latin church, he was shown in New Mexico as a desert hermit in a red mantle, sometimes with a lion or other creature such as a donkey, bird, or lizard. He holds a cross and stone with which he beat himself; a trumpet in an upper corner represents the voice of God, which he heard.

· SAINT JOHN NEPOMUK ·
SAN JUAN NEPOMUCENO

He wears a surplice over a black cassock and a biretta and sometimes a short ermine cape; he holds a cross and palm. Nepomuk was martyred by his king for refusing to break the secrecy of the confessional. The cult spread from Prague, Bohemia, to Mexico. In New Mexico the Penitentes adopted him as a symbol of secrecy.

· SAINT JOSEPH ·
SAN JOSÉ PATRIARCA

*Shown in brightly colored, patterned biblical robes, he holds a flowering
staff and the Christ Child. Sometimes he has a crown and is always bearded.
In New Mexico shown as less aged than typically in European depictions.*

· SAINT LAURENCE ·
SAN LORENZO

A deacon of the early Christian era in Rome, he is said to have been born in Spain. He is shown in deacon's dalmatic, smooth shaven as a rule, holding a martyr's palm and a gridiron, symbol of his death by fire.

· SAINT LIBERATA ·
SANTA LIBRADA

Now declared apocryphal, her cult was a great Spanish devotion for more
than five hundred years. She is portrayed as a crucified woman with long robes
and flowing hair.

· MICHAEL THE ARCHANGEL ·
SAN MIGUEL ARCÁNGEL

The messenger of God and captain of heavenly hosts, he is identified by scales with which he will weigh souls on Judgment Day and a sword or lance with which he subdues a dragon, representing Satan, under his feet. Michael wears a helmet, cuirass, and greaves.

· OUR LADY OF MOUNT CARMEL ·
NUESTRA SEÑORA DEL CARMEN

*This advocation of the Virgin correctly wears a brown flowered robe with a
yellow panel, a crown, and holds the Christ Child and a scapular bearing the
emblem of her confraternity. Sometimes found in red robes. She is the
intercessor for souls in purgatory.*

· THE MOURNING MOTHER ·
NUESTRA SEÑORA DE LA SOLEDAD

New Mexican images that refer to the loneliness (soledad) of the Virgin after the Crucifixion show her in black robes and mantle with a white apron and rosary, sometimes with implements of the Passion. She is frequently, but erroneously, referred to as Our Lady of Solitude.

· SAINT PETER ·

SAN PEDRO APÓSTOL

The gatekeeper of heaven, he is shown as an old man in long robes with a large key in his hand and, rarely, with a rooster beside him.

· RAPHAEL THE ARCHANGEL ·
SAN RAFAEL ARCÁNGEL

The angel who appeared to Tobias and healed his father's blindness by telling him to catch a fish, burn it, and anoint his father's eyes with the ashes that, if he had faith, would cure the blindness. Rafael is shown in pilgrim's tunic and staff, with a gourd for water and carrying a fish.

· SAINT RAYMOND NONNATUS ·
SAN RAMÓN NONATO

*He wears red or orange chasuble or cloak over white robes and holds a
monstrance and wand bearing three crowns, symbols of the earthly honors
that he rejected. A Mercedarian, he spent his life ransoming captive Christians
from Moorish Africa. Because of his cesarean birth he became patron of
midwives in New Mexico.*

· OUR LADY OF REFUGE ·
Nstra Sra REFUGIO DE PECADORES

A half-length, crowned figure with the Infant Christ on her lap. She has a silk scarf around the shoulders and a blue cloak with the cypher MA over it.

· SAINT RITA OF CASCIA ·
SANTA RITA DE CASIA

The cross and skull that she holds, or has near her, distinguish Rita from other saints in black nuns' habits, as does the wound or star on her forehead. She was formerly accredited with granting "the impossible" to her devotees.

· SAINT ROCH ·
SAN ROQUE

A medieval layman who nursed the sick and begged alms for them, he caught the plague himself. Hiding himself in the forest he was healed by the grace of God. His dog licked his sores and brought him bread. He wears a pilgrim's tunic, cloak, and boots, sometimes with cocked hat and staff or with his dog. Other renderings in New Mexico mistakenly show him in blue Franciscan habit.

· SAINT ROSALIE OF PALERMO ·
SANTA ROSALÍA DE PALERMO

Her black, gray, or brown dress, crown of thorny roses, bare feet, and long hair
indicate that Rosalie was a female hermit. She holds a cross or book and con-
templates a skull. She was thought to have ended a great plague in Sicily some
time after her death.

· OUR LADY OF THE ROSARY ·
NUESTRA SEÑORA DEL ROSARIO

*Correctly, this advocation should show the Virgin holding the Child while she
gives a rosary to Saint Dominic, but in New Mexico some images show only
the crowned Virgin and rosary. Garments are often red with a small jacket but
also may be blue and white or other colors.*

· OUR LADY OF SAINT JOHN OF THE LAKES ·
Nstra Sra DE SAN JUAN
DE LOS LAGOS

These are statue images after a miraculous statue in the town of the above name in Jalisco, Mexico. Identified by a jeweled crown, hoop skirt, and pair of tall candles by her.

· OUR LADY OF SORROWS ·
NUESTRA SEÑORA DE LOS DOLORES

An allegorical figure symbolizing the seven sorrows in the life of Mary and the most popular of all images of her in New Mexico. She wears a red robe and blue mantle, with one or more swords in her breast, and wrings her hands.

· THE FRANCISCAN SHIELD ·

The crossed arms symbolize Christ and Saint Francis of Assisi. This emblem is found on altar screens in the New Mexico churches of Ranchos de Taos, Trampas, and the Santuario de Chimayó.

• S U G G E S T E D   R E A D I N G •

Books on Christian Iconography and Lives of the Saints

Butler, Alban
1987   *Butler's Lives of Patron Saints*. Harper & Row, San Francisco.

Drake, Maurice and Wilfred
1971   *Saints and Their Emblems*. Lenox Hill Publishing & Dist. Co.,
New York.

Duchet-Suchaux, and Pastoureau, Michel
1994   *The Bible and the Saints*. Flammarion, Paris-New York.

Ferguson, George
1967   *Signs and Symbols in Christian Art*. Oxford University Press,
New York.

Ferrando Roig, Juan
1950   *Iconografía de los Santos*. Ediciones Omega S.A., Barcelona.

Hall, James
1974   *Dictionary of Subjects & Symbols in Art*. Harper & Row,
New York.

Jameson, Anna Brownell (Murphy)
1890 *The History of Our Lord.* Longmans, Green, and Co., London.

1890 *Legends of the Madonna.* Longmans, Green, and Co., London.

1896 *Legends of the Monastic Orders.* Houghton, Mifflin and Co., Boston and New York.

1896 *Sacred and Legendary Art.* Houghton, Mifflin and Co., Boston and New York.

Lange, Yvonne
1978 "Santo Niño de Atocha: A Mexican Cult Is Transplanted to Spain." *El Palacio* 84 (4) (Winter 1978), 2–7.

1991 "The Impact of European Prints on the Devotional Tin Paintings of Mexico: A Transferral Hypothesis." In *The Art of Private Devotion: Retablo Painting of Mexico,* ed. Gloria Giffords, 64–72. InterCultura, Fort Worth.

Lerner, Ernst
1950 *Symbols, Signs & Signets.* World Publishing Co., Cleveland and New York.

Réau, Louis
1955–59 *Iconographie de l'Art Chrétien.* Presses Universitaires de France, Paris.

Schiller, Gertrud
1971 *Iconography of Christian Art.* Trans. Janet Seligman. New York Graphic Society, Greenwich, Conn.

Steele, Thomas J., S.J.
1994 *Santos and Saints: The Religious Folk Art of Hispanic New Mexico,* rev. ed. Ancient City Press, Santa Fe, N.M.

Trens, Manuel
1947 *María, Iconografía de la Virgen en el Arte Español.* Editorial Plus-Ultra, Madrid.

Voragine, Jacobus de
1993 *The Golden Legend: Readings on the Saints.* Princeton University Press, Princeton, N.J.